A DAY IN THE LIFE OF A

BASEBALL PLAYER

MO VAUGHN

by **ERIC ARNOLD**
Photographs by Ilene Perlman

SCHOLASTIC INC.
New York Toronto London Auckland Sydney

A roaring cheer and deepest appreciation to Mo Vaughn
for his time and commitment to this book project.
Many thanks to the Boston Red Sox Baseball Club, with special thanks to Dick
Bresciani, Kevin Shea, Steve August, Mary Jane Ryan, and Adam Levin.
Thanks to Mark Gillam, Rick Parsons, Shirley and Leroy Vaughn,
and Roosevelt Smith and Bryan Wilson
of the Mo Vaughn Youth Development Program.

In loving memory of my parents, Esther and Irv.
For Christen and our MVP's Tali and Gabriel, and for Ben and Adam.
To Heidi Kilgras: Warmest thanks for your hard work, humor, and support.
Special thanks to Juwanda Ford, Kristina Iulo, and Kate Waters.
— E.A.

For my nephew Christopher; may his dreams come true.
To my family for their love and support.
To Jane for those wonderful baseball tips.
— I.P.

Photo Credit:
p.7: Photo by Steve Gilbert/Studioflex Productions.
Used with permission. All rights reserved.
Every effort has been made by the publisher to
locate the owner of the trademarked material used
in this book and to secure the necessary permission.

ISBN 0-590-54350-4

12 11 10 9 8 7 6 5 4 3 2 1   6 7 8 9/9 0 1/0

Printed in the U.S.A.   09

First Scholastic printing, March 1996

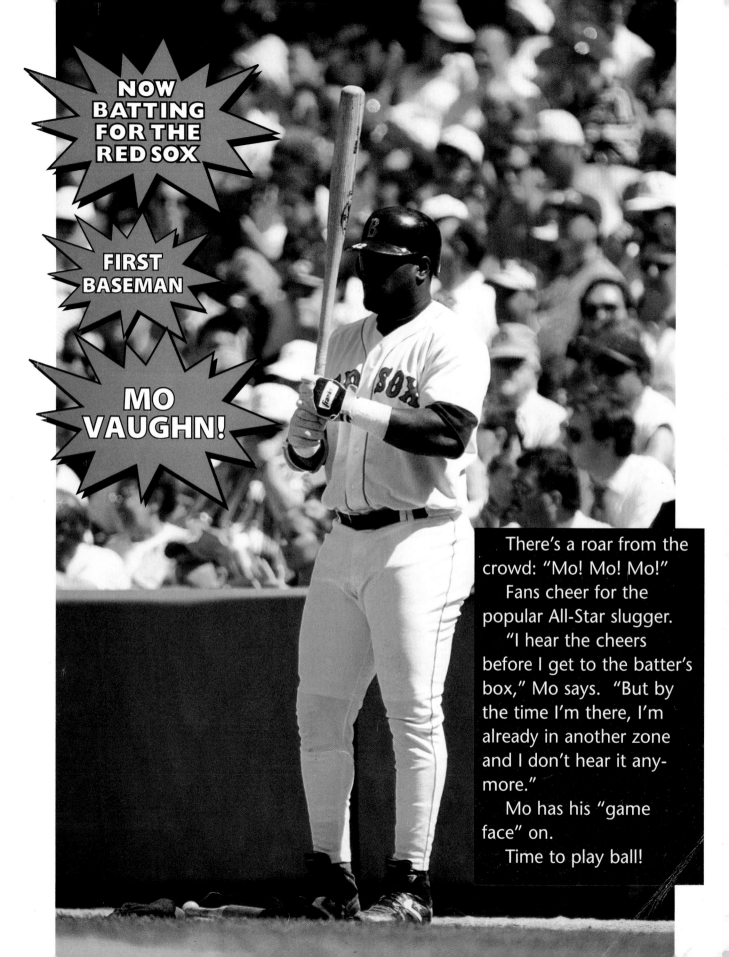

NOW BATTING FOR THE RED SOX

FIRST BASEMAN

MO VAUGHN!

There's a roar from the crowd: "Mo! Mo! Mo!" Fans cheer for the popular All-Star slugger.

"I hear the cheers before I get to the batter's box," Mo says. "But by the time I'm there, I'm already in another zone and I don't hear it anymore."

Mo has his "game face" on.

Time to play ball!

At 6'1", 245 pounds, Mo is a mountain of a man. With powerful arms and legs, and a very serious look, he seems bigger than life. Mo's big heart has also captured the attention of baseball fans.

Living in the Boston area year-round, he donates time and energy to charities and activities for children. "You just don't go through life for yourself, you do for others as well. I use the tools that I have as a professional athlete to enrich the lives of young people."

Mo is a power hitter and a team leader in home runs and runs batted in. He is a valuable player on the Red Sox roster.

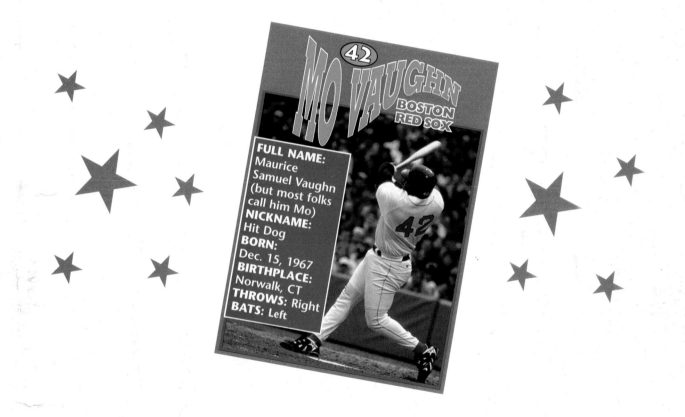

Among his biggest fans are his family. He has two older sisters, Donna and Catherine. His dad, Leroy, worked as a school principal and played professional football with the Baltimore Colts, and his mother, Shirley, worked as a teacher.

You can bet Mo kept up with his schoolwork growing up in that family!

Mo visits schools, hospitals, and libraries to talk and read with kids. He started an afterschool program in a youth center and once took 250 kids to see the Boston Ballet's performance of *The Nutcracker*. In 1994, *Sports Illustrated for Kids* honored Mo by presenting him with the Good Sport Award.

On April 24, 1993, Mo took a phone call from a young fan who tracked him down in California with the help of a Sox radio announcer. Jason Leader, a cancer patient in Boston's Children's Hospital, had a wish for his eleventh birthday — to talk with Mo, his favorite player.

The Red Sox were playing the Angels, and Mo was in the middle of a batting slump. "When I was on the phone with Jason, he was joking and laughing and I said to myself, 'I have nothing to complain about in my everyday life. My problems are really not that big compared to these kids who are faced with death.' I told him to stay strong and I'd try to hit a home run for him that night." In Mo's third at bat, he blasted a homer over the fence in right-center field.

Mo invited Jason to his next home game and asked him to throw out the first pitch — to the glove of his new friend, Mo Vaughn.

The crowd gave Jason a standing ovation.

Baseball is the main thing on Mo's mind during the long 162-game season. Most of the games are played at night, and when he gets home he sometimes has trouble sleeping. He's already thinking about the next pitcher he'll be facing, what strategies worked in the last game, or how he can improve his performance. He often doesn't get to bed until 3:00 in the morning and plays computer games until he gets tired.

Mo gets up early when he has to play a day game. "I don't want to do anything before a game but hang out, because I want to stay mentally focused."

At 6'1", 245 pounds, Mo is a mountain of a man. With powerful arms and legs, and a very serious look, he seems bigger than life. Mo's big heart has also captured the attention of baseball fans.

Living in the Boston area year-round, he donates time and energy to charities and activities for children. "You just don't go through life for yourself, you do for others as well. I use the tools that I have as a professional athlete to enrich the lives of young people."

Mo is a power hitter and a team leader in home runs and runs batted in. He is a valuable player on the Red Sox roster.

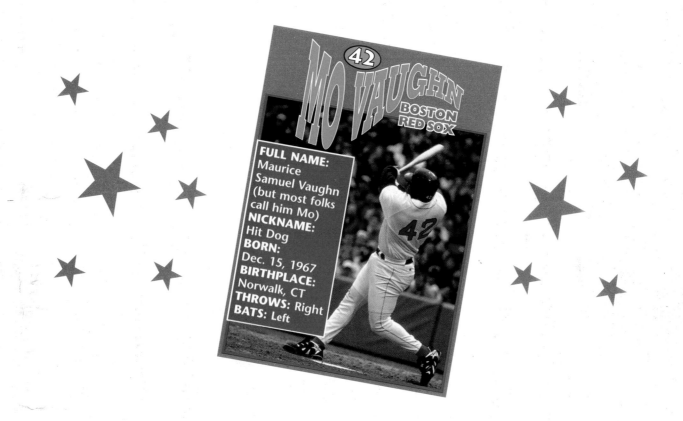

FULL NAME: Maurice Samuel Vaughn (but most folks call him Mo)
NICKNAME: Hit Dog
BORN: Dec. 15, 1967
BIRTHPLACE: Norwalk, CT
THROWS: Right
BATS: Left

Among his biggest fans are his family. He has two older sisters, Donna and Catherine. His dad, Leroy, worked as a school principal and played professional football with the Baltimore Colts, and his mother, Shirley, worked as a teacher.

You can bet Mo kept up with his schoolwork growing up in that family!

Mo visits schools, hospitals, and libraries to talk and read with kids. He started an afterschool program in a youth center and once took 250 kids to see the Boston Ballet's performance of *The Nutcracker*. In 1994, *Sports Illustrated for Kids* honored Mo by presenting him with the Good Sport Award.

On April 24, 1993, Mo took a phone call from a young fan who tracked him down in California with the help of a Sox radio announcer. Jason Leader, a cancer patient in Boston's Children's Hospital, had a wish for his eleventh birthday — to talk with Mo, his favorite player.

The Red Sox were playing the Angels, and Mo was in the middle of a batting slump. "When I was on the phone with Jason, he was joking and laughing and I said to myself, 'I have nothing to complain about in my everyday life. My problems are really not that big compared to these kids who are faced with death.' I told him to stay strong and I'd try to hit a home run for him that night." In Mo's third at bat, he blasted a homer over the fence in right-center field.

Mo invited Jason to his next home game and asked him to throw out the first pitch — to the glove of his new friend, Mo Vaughn.

The crowd gave Jason a standing ovation.

For breakfast, Mo chooses from nearly ten different cereal brands on his kitchen counter. His favorite cereal is Life®.

"I read the paper every morning to find out where the Red Sox are in the standings and what we need to do to get to the top." After breakfast, Mo will either go back to sleep for a little while, read, watch hitting videos or sports news, or talk on the phone. In the off-season, Mo had to change his phone number eight times because so many people were calling him to donate time to different causes. But if it has to do with kids, it's often hard for him to say no.

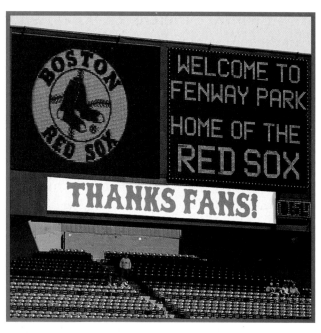

The Red Sox play their home games at Fenway Park. Mo drives himself to the ballpark and always tries to get there early. For a day game, he arrives at the park by 9:30 A.M. All players must be dressed for batting practice by 10:30 A.M.

At Fenway, there is a clubhouse for the Red Sox players, and that's where Mo's locker is. There is also a clubhouse for the visiting team.

"I've got the messiest locker in the entire world. Inside, I've got pictures of places I've been, cards, and photographs of myself with my favorite players. I keep pens, pieces of paper, books, spikes — anything that has been given to me. I've got T-shirts in there that I've had since college! They're all lined up, and even though I might not use them, it's important for me that they be there. All of the things in my locker are like a diary of everything I've done."

But look how neat his closet is at home! There's even a matching tie hanging with each suit.

Time to get ready for BP (batting practice) and the start of a three-game series with the Chicago White Sox. The Red Sox are the home team, and take the field first.

"My uniform dress for BP is really raggedy. I usually wear a hat or helmet, and sunglasses. I put on some old dirty socks, a pair of sneakers left untied, and some really loose pants. My T-shirt sleeves and collar are cut off, and my shirt-tail is dragging — just so that I am not in a serious frame of mind. The time to be serious is at game time."

On a cool day, Mo often wears his knit Red Sox hat for BP. But even on a hot day, he may wear long sleeves. "I have to be warm all the time, even if it's 80 degrees!" When Mo is warm, his bat is hot!

At the start of BP, the team does pregame warm-ups, which include running in the outfield and stretching.

The players line up for a game of "long toss" while listening to music blaring on the loudspeakers. They get to choose the songs they would like to hear during batting practice.

Mo practices hard during BP, but he still tries to have fun. After long toss, Mo might field ground balls at third base, run more laps in the outfield, or talk with teammates. Mo walks toward the dugout with ace pitcher Roger Clemens. This is also a time when team members can talk with reporters from newspapers, radio, or television.

Mo practices hard during BP, but he still tries to have fun. After long toss, Mo might field ground balls at third base, run more laps in the outfield, or talk with teammates. Mo walks toward the dugout with ace pitcher Roger Clemens. This is also a time when team members can talk with reporters from newspapers, radio, or television.

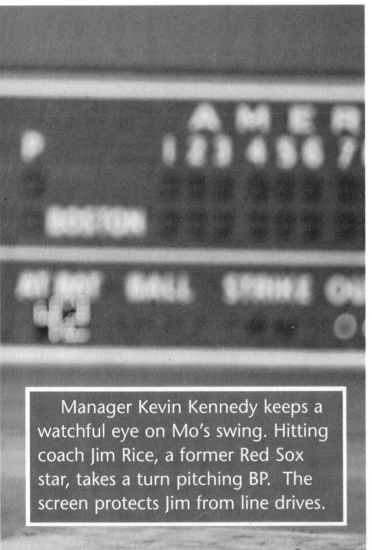

During a player's turn in the batting cage, he practices hitting base hits, home runs, and bunts. The next batter up fields the bunts.

An important hitting drill is the "hit and run." A player gets to practice both placing a hit and baserunning. When a player finishes his turn at bat, he waits near the cage for the next batter to come up. He sprints down the baseline to first base when the batter takes his first swing. The runner stays on first base while the new batter tries to get him to second base by placing a hit through the infield.

Mo always puts in extra time in the batting cage. "It's something that has made me into the type of hitter I am today."

Mo credits his dad for his work habits. "My dad told me that I've got to work harder than anybody else. I'm a talented athlete, don't get me wrong, but I'm not the fastest and I'm not the strongest. I just work harder than most guys in a game."

Fellow slugger Jose Canseco practices the "flip drill," which is designed to increase arm strength. A player flips the ball to the batter, who swings at it with either one or two hands on the bat.

Did you ever wonder what happens to a broken bat? At Fenway Park, it looks as if the players plant them during batting practice. . . .

The left field wall is famous as the "Green Monster." It is 310 feet down the third base line and 37 feet high — a perfect target for the Hit Dog and his big bat. "My bat is very important — it's my tool, like a pen is to a writer. I use a heavy bat — thirty-six inches, thirty-six ounces."

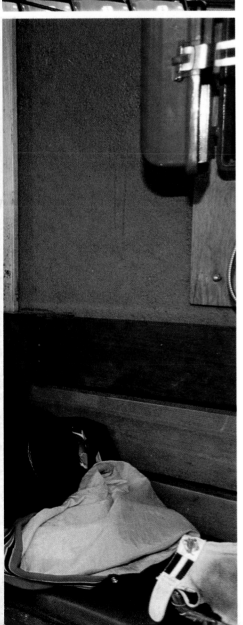

It's pretty quiet in the park except for the activity on the field. People who work at Fenway sometimes watch batting practice before it's time to work. Fans are allowed into the ballpark an hour and a half before game time to watch BP.

It's a good time for Mo to grab a quiet moment for himself in the dugout. During a game the dugout is anything but quiet: "We talk about the game and the strategy we need in order to win. We also try to keep guys 'up' if they are not hitting well. Not everybody is going to be hitting well all of the time, and it's important that they not lose their confidence."

Keeping a positive attitude is key to Mo. "If a game isn't going well — if I'm 0 for 3 — I always say to myself, 'I'm just one pitch away from getting a hit tonight.' That's how you've got to think about it — you'll get that pitch and hit!"

Mo knows he's got to stay focused. "I don't get that excited over home runs. I come back and give everybody handshakes, but I'm already thinking about my next at bat. There's really no time to celebrate in baseball. As fast as you become the hero one night, you might strike out and lose the game the next night."

Mo's quiet time doesn't last long. . . .

It's pretty quiet in the park except for the activity on the field. People who work at Fenway sometimes watch batting practice before it's time to work. Fans are allowed into the ballpark an hour and a half before game time to watch BP.

It's a good time for Mo to grab a quiet moment for himself in the dugout. During a game the dugout is anything but quiet: "We talk about the game and the strategy we need in order to win. We also try to keep guys 'up' if they are not hitting well. Not everybody is going to be hitting well all of the time, and it's important that they not lose their confidence."

Keeping a positive attitude is key to Mo. "If a game isn't going well — if I'm 0 for 3 — I always say to myself, 'I'm just one pitch away from getting a hit tonight.' That's how you've got to think about it — you'll get that pitch and hit!"

Mo knows he's got to stay focused. "I don't get that excited over home runs. I come back and give everybody handshakes, but I'm already thinking about my next at bat. There's really no time to celebrate in baseball. As fast as you become the hero one night, you might strike out and lose the game the next night."

Mo's quiet time doesn't last long. . . .

And Mo, being Mo, takes the time to sign autographs for his fans. Mo also gets many requests for autographs mailed to him at Fenway. "I give them to my parents. They open the letters and have everything ready for me to sign. I usually do that once a week before a game."

Now the White Sox take the field for BP. Leading the way is their star first baseman, Frank Thomas, whose nickname is "the Big Hurt."

"I respect my friends in the game, like Frank Thomas and Cecil Fielder, to name a few. We are all tight. I also respect the older guys — Paul Molitor, Mark McGwire, Don Mattingly — for their skill, how long they have played, and what they bring to the game. There are not enough young players who pick the brains of these talented athletes as I do in order to learn."

While the White Sox take their BP, Mo heads back to the clubhouse (no cameras allowed!).

"I always take a shower after BP. If I had a bad batting practice, it helps to shower and wash it off. Also, if the weather is hot and sticky during BP, I want to wash that dirt off of me. Once I take a shower, I feel new again and refreshed. I'm ready to go!"

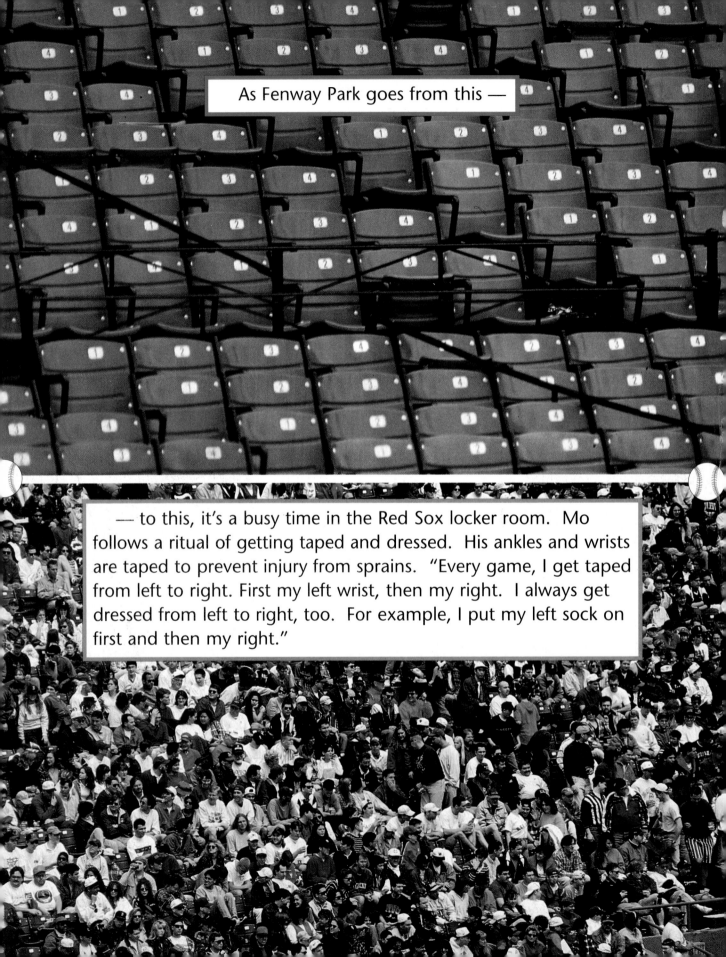

As Fenway Park goes from this —

— to this, it's a busy time in the Red Sox locker room. Mo follows a ritual of getting taped and dressed. His ankles and wrists are taped to prevent injury from sprains. "Every game, I get taped from left to right. First my left wrist, then my right. I always get dressed from left to right, too. For example, I put my left sock on first and then my right."

Before the game, the Red Sox meet to go over the scouting report on the White Sox, since it's the first time the two teams have met this season. The manager talks to the players about the hitting styles of the White Sox players.

Meanwhile, the Fenway ground crew prepares the infield dirt one last time so that it's flat and unmarked for the game.

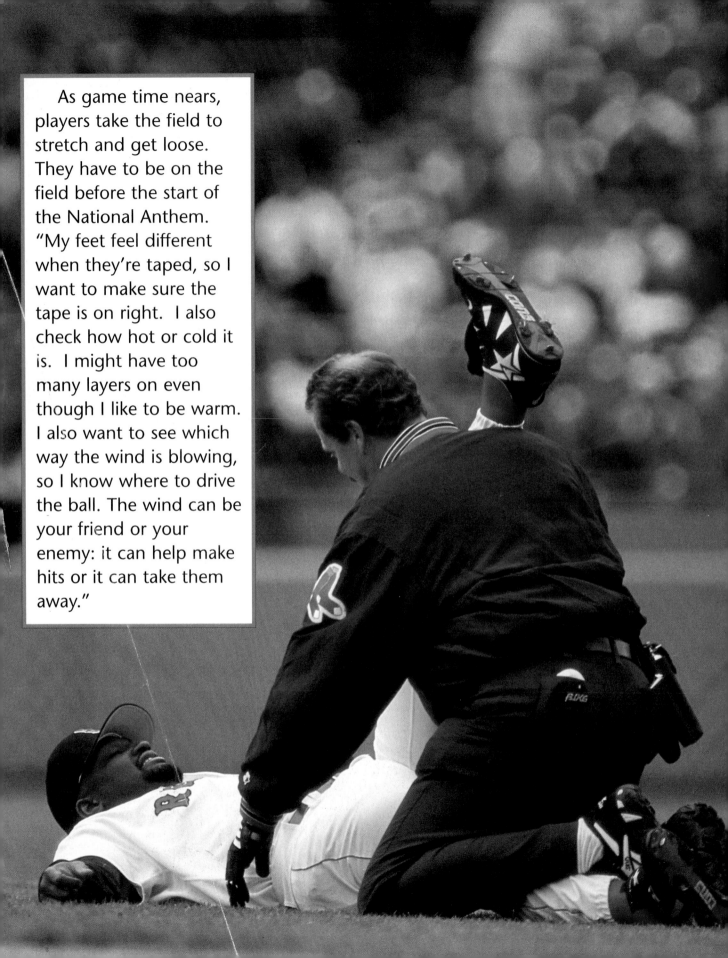

As game time nears, players take the field to stretch and get loose. They have to be on the field before the start of the National Anthem. "My feet feel different when they're taped, so I want to make sure the tape is on right. I also check how hot or cold it is. I might have too many layers on even though I like to be warm. I also want to see which way the wind is blowing, so I know where to drive the ball. The wind can be your friend or your enemy: it can help make hits or it can take them away."

And there are more autographs to sign!
Mo heads into the dugout and down the ramp to the clubhouse once more before game time.

It might look as if the Red Sox have some very young players on their team, but these are the winners of today's fan contest. It's very exciting for them to sit in the dugout before the game.

Wearing their home field "whites," the real Red Sox line up for the National Anthem. Before the anthem ends, the crowd begins to cheer and Fenway comes alive!

"Your eyes light up," says Mo. "It's like something just clicks. It's game time!"

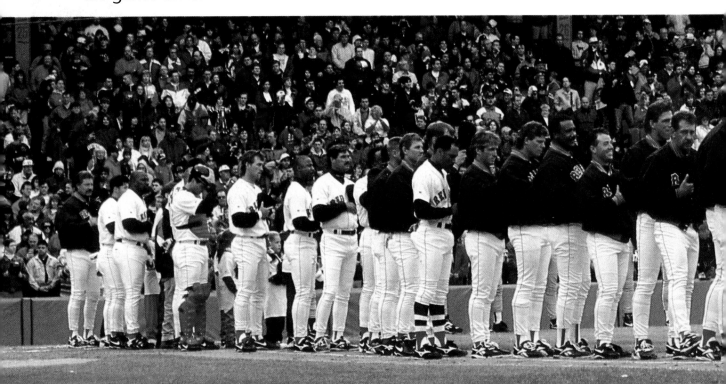

Mo's parents live in Virginia, but they try to get to all the games the Red Sox play in the northeastern part of the United States. It means a lot to Mo to see his family in the stands cheering him on. After all, it was Mo's mom who first taught him how to hit a baseball when he was two years old. "My dad was busy with work, so my mother taught me how to hit left-handed because she was left-handed. I was naturally a righty."

During the game, Mo uses the fundamentals he learned as a young ballplayer, which are just as important to a professional ballplayer:

FIELDING: "You've got to move your feet, keep your glove down, get your butt down, and with your hands out in front, you 'look' the ball into your glove. Whenever you pick up the ball with your glove hand, your front foot should come up to where the ball was.

That means you're going up through the ball and ready for the next move."

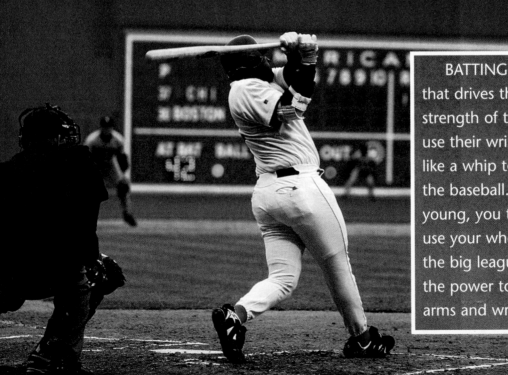

BATTING: "It's bat speed that drives the baseball, not the strength of the player. Batters use their wrists to snap the bat like a whip to apply pressure to the baseball. When you're young, you think you've got to use your whole body to hit. In the big leagues, you learn that the power to hit is all in your arms and wrists."

The Red Sox won the game, and the team lines up to shake hands. After the game, players rush to get showered and dressed, and talk with reporters.

Mo walks through the clubhouse exit leading to the players' parking lot, where his parents and relatives are waiting for him. And Mo is already thinking about tomorrow's game.

"I love the game of baseball. There's only one way to play — respect the game and hustle through each play." Respect is an important word to Mo.

"When I was at Seton Hall University, my college coach made me promise that if I ever got to the big leagues, I would wear number forty-two, the number Jackie Robinson wore. And that's what I did."

Mo wears number 42 to honor Jackie Robinson, the first African-American to play in the major leagues.